THE LEARNED WOMEN

by

MOLIÈRE

THE LEARNED WOMEN
(Les Femmes Savantes)

by
MOLIÈRE

Translated into English prose
by
Charles Heron Wall

Edited by
B. K. De Fabris

TIMELESS📖CLASSICS

PERSONS REPRESENTED:

CHRYSALE, *an honest bourgeois*
PHILAMINTE, *wife to* CHRYSALE
ARMANDE & HENRIETTE, *their daughters*
ARISTE, *brother to* CHRYSALE
BÉLISE, *his sister*
CLITANDRE, *lover to* HENRIETTE
TRISSOTIN, *a wit*
VADIUS, *a learned man*
MARTINE, *a kitchen-maid*
LÉPINE, *servant to* CHRYSALE
JULIEN, *servant to* VADIUS
A NOTARY.

*The comedy of 'Les Femmes Savantes' was acted on March 11,
1692. Molière acted the part of Chrysale.*

ACT I.

SCENE I.
ARMANDE, HENRIETTE.

ARMANDE: What! Sister, you will give up the sweet and enchanting title of maiden? You can entertain thoughts of marrying! This vulgar wish can enter your head!

HENRIETTE: Yes, sister.

ARMANDE: Ah! Who can bear that "yes"? Can anyone hear it without feelings of disgust?

HENRIETTE: What is there in marriage which can oblige you, sister, to....

ARMANDE: Ah! Fie!

HENRIETTE: What?

ARMANDE: Fie! I tell you. Can you not conceive what offence the very mention of such a word presents to the imagination, and what a repulsive image it offers to the thoughts? Do you not shudder before it? And can you bring yourself to accept all the consequences which this word implies?

HENRIETTE: When I consider all the consequences which this word implies, I only have offered to my thoughts a husband, children, and a home; and I see nothing in all this to defile the imagination, or to make one shudder.

ARMANDE: O heavens! Can such ties have charms for you?

HENRIETTE: And what at my age can I do better than take a husband who loves me, and whom I love, and through such a tender union secure the delights of an innocent life? If there be conformity of tastes, do you see no attraction in such a bond?

ARMANDE: Ah! heavens! What a grovelling disposition! What a poor part you act in the world, to confine yourself to family affairs, and to think of no more soul-stirring pleasures than those offered by an idol of a husband and by brats of children! Leave these base pleasures to the low and vulgar. Raise your thoughts to more exalted objects; endeavour to cultivate a taste for nobler pursuits; and treating sense and matter with contempt, give yourself, as we do, wholly to the cultivation of your mind. You have for an example our mother, who is everywhere honoured with the name of learned. Try, as we do, to prove yourself her daughter; aspire to the enlightened intellectuality which is found in our family, and acquire a taste for the rapturous pleasures which the love of study brings to the heart and mind. Instead of being in bondage to the will of a man, marry yourself, sister, to philosophy, for it alone raises you above the rest of mankind, gives sovereign empire to reason, and submits to its laws the animal part, with those groveling desires which lower us to the level of the brute. These are the gentle flames, the sweet ties, which should fill every moment of life. And the cares to which I see so many women given up, appear to me pitiable frivolities.

HENRIETTE: Heaven, whose will is supreme, forms us at our birth to fill different spheres; and it is not every mind which is composed of materials fit to make a philosopher. If your mind is created to soar to those heights which are attained by the speculations of learned men, mine is fitted, sister, to take a meaner flight and to centre its weakness on the petty cares of the world. Let us not interfere with the just decrees of Heaven; but let each of us follow our different instincts. You, borne on the wings of a great and noble genius, will inhabit the lofty regions of philosophy; I, remaining here below, will taste the terrestrial charms of matrimony. Thus, in our several paths, we shall still imitate our mother: you, in her mind and its noble longings; I, in her grosser senses and coarser pleasures; you, in the productions of genius and light, and I, sister, in productions more material.

ARMANDE: When we wish to take a person for a model, it is the nobler side we should imitate; and it is not taking our mother for a model, sister, to cough and spit like her.

HENRIETTE: But you would not have been what you boast yourself to be if our mother had had only her nobler qualities; and well it is for you that her lofty genius did not always devote itself to philosophy. Pray, leave me to those littlenesses to which you owe life, and do not, by wishing me to imitate you, deny some little savant entrance into the world.

ARMANDE: I see that you cannot be cured of the foolish infatuation of taking a husband to yourself. But, pray, let us know whom you intend to marry; I suppose that you do not aim at Clitandre?

HENRIETTE: And why should I not? Does he lack merit? Is it a low choice I have made?

ARMANDE: Certainly not; but it would not be honest to take away the conquest of another; and it is a fact not unknown to the world that Clitandre has publicly sighed for me.

HENRIETTE: Yes; but all those sighs are mere vanities for you; you do not share human weaknesses; your mind has for ever renounced matrimony, and philosophy has all your love. Thus, having in your heart no pretensions to Clitandre, what does it matter to you if another has such pretensions?

ARMANDE: The empire which reason holds over the senses does not call upon us to renounce the pleasure of adulation; and we may refuse for a husband a man of merit whom we would willingly see swell the number of our admirers.

HENRIETTE: I have not prevented him from continuing his worship, but have only received the homage of his passion when you had rejected it.

ARMANDE: But do you find entire safety, tell me, in the vows of a rejected lover? Do you think his passion for you so great that all love for me can be dead in his heart?

HENRIETTE: He tells me so, sister, and I trust him.

ARMANDE: Do not, sister, be so ready to trust him; and be sure that, when he says he gives me up and loves you, he really does not mean it, but deceives himself.

HENRIETTE: I cannot say; but if you wish it, it will be easy for us to discover the true state of things. I see him coming, and on this point he will be sure to give us full information.

SCENE II.
CLITANDRE, ARMANDE, HENRIETTE.

HENRIETTE: Clitandre, deliver me from a doubt my sister has raised in me. Pray open your heart to us; tell us the truth, and let us know which of us has a claim upon your love.

ARMANDE: No, no; I will not force upon your love the hardship of an explanation. I have too much respect for others, and know how perplexing it is to make an open avowal before witnesses.

CLITANDRE: No; my heart cannot dissemble, and it is no hardship to me to speak openly. Such a step in no way perplexes me, and I acknowledge before all, freely and openly, that the tender chains which bind me *(pointing to HENRIETTE)*, my homage and my love, are all on this side. Such a confession can cause you no surprise, for you wished things to be thus. I was touched by your attractions, and my tender sighs told you enough of my ardent desires; my heart offered you an immortal love, but you did not think the conquest which your eyes had made noble enough. I have suffered many slights, for you reigned over my heart like a tyrant; but weary at last with so much pain, I looked elsewhere for a conqueror more gentle, and for chains less cruel. *(Pointing to HENRIETTE)* I have met with them here, and my bonds will forever be precious to me. These eyes have looked upon me with compassion, and have dried my tears. They have not despised what you had refused. Such kindness has captivated me, and there is nothing which would now break my chains. Therefore I beseech you, Madam, never to make an attempt to regain a heart which has resolved to die in this gentle bondage.

ARMANDE: Bless me, Sir, who told you that I had such a desire, and, in short, that I cared so much for you? I think it tolerably ridiculous that you should imagine such a thing, and very impertinent in you to declare it to me.

HENRIETTE: Ah! gently, sister. Where is now that moral sense which has so much power over that which is merely animal in us, and which can restrain the madness of anger?

ARMANDE: And you, who speak to me, what moral sense have you when you respond to a love which is offered to you before you have received leave from those who have given you birth? Know that duty subjects you to their laws, and that you may love only in accordance with their choice; for they have a supreme authority over your heart, and it is criminal in you to dispose of it yourself.

HENRIETTE: I thank you for the great kindness you show me in teaching me my duty. My heart intends to follow the line of conduct you have traced; and to show you that I profit by your advice, pray, Clitandre, see that your love is strengthened by the consent of those from whom I have received birth. Acquire thus a right over my wishes, and for me the power of loving you without a crime.

CLITANDRE: I will do so with all diligence. I only waited for this kind permission from you.

ARMANDE: You triumph, sister, and seem to fancy that you thereby give me pain.

HENRIETTE: I, sister? By no means. I know that the laws of reason will always have full power over your senses, and that, through the lessons you derive from wisdom, you are altogether above such weakness. Far from thinking you moved by any vexation, I believe that you will use your influence to help me, will second his demand of my hand, and will by your approbation hasten the happy day of our marriage. I beseech you to do so; and in order to secure this end....

ARMANDE: Your little mind thinks it grand to resort to raillery, and you seem wonderfully proud of a heart which I abandon to you.

HENRIETTE: Abandoned it may be; yet this heart, sister, is not so disliked by you but that, if you could regain it by stooping, you would even condescend to do so.

ARMANDE: I scorn to answer such foolish prating.

HENRIETTE: You do well; and you show us inconceivable moderation.

SCENE III.
CLITANDRE, HENRIETTE.

HENRIETTE: Your frank confession has rather taken her aback.

CLITANDRE: She deserves such freedom of speech, and all the haughtiness of her proud folly merits my outspokenness! But since you give me leave, I will go to your father, to....

HENRIETTE: The safest thing to do would be to gain my mother over. My father easily consents to everything, but he places little weight on what he himself resolves. He has received from Heaven a certain gentleness which makes him readily submit to the will of his wife. It is she who governs, and who in a dictatorial tone lays down the law whenever she has made up her mind to anything. I wish I could see in you a more pliant spirit towards her and towards my aunt. If you would but fall in with their views, you would secure their favour and their esteem.

CLITANDRE: I am so sincere that I can never bring myself to praise, even in your sister, that side of her character which resembles theirs. Female doctors are not to my taste. I like a woman to have some knowledge of everything; but I cannot admire in her the revolting passion of wishing to be clever for the mere sake of being clever. I prefer that she should, at times, affect ignorance of what she really knows. In short, I like her to hide her knowledge, and to be learned without publishing her learning abroad, quoting the authors, making use of pompous words, and being witty under the least provocation. I greatly respect your mother, but I cannot approve her wild fancies, nor make myself an echo of what she says. I cannot support the praises she bestows upon that literary hero of hers, Mr. Trissotin, who vexes and wearies me to death. I cannot bear to see her have any esteem for such a man, and to see her reckon among men of genius a fool whose writings are everywhere hissed; a pedant whose liberal pen furnishes all the markets with wastepaper.

HENRIETTE: His writings, his speeches, in short, everything in him is unpleasant to me; and I feel towards him as you do. But as he possesses great ascendancy over my mother, you must force yourself to yield somewhat. A lover should make his court where his heart is engaged; he should win the favour of everyone; and in order to have nobody opposed to his love, try to please even the dog of the house.

CLITANDRE: Yes, you are right; but Mr. Trissotin is hateful to me. I cannot consent, in order to win his favour, to dishonour myself by praising his works. It is through them that he was first brought to my notice, and I knew him before I had seen him. I saw in the trash which he writes all that his pedantic person everywhere shows forth; the persistent haughtiness of his presumption, the intrepidity of the good opinion he has of his person, the calm overweening confidence which at all times makes him so satisfied with himself, and with the writings of which he boasts; so that he would not exchange his renown for all the honours of the greatest general.

HENRIETTE: You have good eyes to see all that.

CLITANDRE: I even guessed what he was like; and by means of the verses with which he deluges us, I saw what the poet must be. So well had I pictured to myself all his features and gait that one day, meeting a man in the galleries of the Palace of Justice [footnote: the resort of the best company in those days.], I laid a wager that it must be Trissotin—and I won my wager.

HENRIETTE: What a tale!

CLITANDRE: No, I assure you that it is the perfect truth. But I see your aunt coming; allow me, I pray you, to tell her of the longings of my heart, and to gain her kind help with your mother.

SCENE IV.
BÉLISE, CLITANDRE.

CLITANDRE: Suffer a lover, Madam, to profit by such a propitious moment to reveal to you his sincere devotion....

BELISE: Ah! gently! Beware of opening your heart too freely to me; although I have placed you in the list of my lovers, you must use no interpreter but your eyes, and never explain by another language desires which are an insult to me. Love me; sigh for me; burn for my charms; but let me know nothing of it. I can shut my eyes to your secret flame, as long as you keep yourself to dumb interpreters; but if your mouth meddle in the matter, I must for ever banish you from my sight.

CLITANDRE: Do not be alarmed at the intentions of my heart. Henriette is, Madam, the object of my love, and I come ardently to conjure you to favour the love I have for her.

BELISE: Ah! truly now, the subterfuge shows excellent wit. This subtle evasion deserves praise; and in all the romances I have glanced over, I have never met with anything more ingenious.

CLITANDRE: This is no attempt at wit, Madam; it is the avowal of what my heart feels. Heaven has bound me to the beauty of Henriette by the ties of an unchangeable love. Henriette holds me in her lovely chains; and to marry Henriette is the end of all my hopes. You can do much towards it; and what I have come to ask you is that you will condescend to second my addresses.

BELISE: I see the end to which your demand would gently head, and I understand whom you mean under that name. The metaphor is clever; and not to depart from it, let me tell you that Henriette rebels against matrimony, and that you must love her without any hope of having your love returned.

CLITANDRE: But, Madam, what is the use of such a perplexing debate? Why will you persist in believing what is not?

BELISE: Dear me! Do not trouble yourself so much. Leave off denying what your looks have often made me understand. Let it suffice that I am content with the subterfuge your love has so skilfully adopted, and that under the figure to which respect has limited it, I am willing to suffer its homage; always provided that its transports, guided by honour, offer only pure vows on my altars.

CLITANDRE: But....

BELISE: Farewell. This ought really to satisfy you, and I have said more than I wished to say.

CLITANDRE: But your error....

BELISE: Leave me. I am blushing now; and my modesty has had much to bear.

CLITANDRE: May I be hanged if I love you; and....

BELISE: No, no. I will hear nothing more.

SCENE V.
CLITANDRE *(alone)*

CLITANDRE: Deuce take the foolish woman with her dreams! Was anything so preposterous ever heard of? I must go and ask the help of a person of more sense.

ACT II.

SCENE I.

ARISTE *(leaving CLITANDRE, and still speaking to him).*

ARISTE: Yes; I will bring you an answer as soon as I can. I will press, insist, do all that should be done. How many things a lover has to say when one would suffice; and how impatient he is for all that he desires! Never....

SCENE II
CHRYSALE, ARISTE.

ARISTE: Good day to you, brother.

CHRYSALE: And to you also, brother.

ARISTE: Do you know what brings me here?

CHRYSALE: No, I do not; but I am ready to hear it, if it pleases you to tell me.

ARISTE: You have known Clitandre for some time now?

CHRYSALE: Certainly; and he often comes to our house.

ARISTE: And what do you think of him?

CHRYSALE: I think him to be a man of honour, wit, courage, and uprightness, and I know very few people who have more merit.

ARISTE: A certain wish of his has brought me here; and I am glad to see the esteem you have for him.

CHRYSALE: I became acquainted with his late father when I was in Rome.

ARISTE: Ah!

CHRYSALE: He was a perfect gentleman.

ARISTE: So it is said.

CHRYSALE: We were only about twenty-eight years of age, and, upon my word, we were, both of us, very gay young fellows.

ARISTE: I believe it.

CHRYSALE: We greatly affected the Roman ladies, and everybody there spoke of our pranks. We made many people jealous, I can tell you.

ARISTE: Excellent; but let us come to what brings me here.

SCENE III.

BÉLISE *(entering softly and listening)*, CHRYSALE, ARISTE.

ARISTE: Clitandre has chosen me to be his interpreter to you; he has fallen in love with Henriette.

CHRYSALE: What! with my daughter?

ARISTE: Yes. Clitandre is delighted with her, and you never saw a lover so smitten!

BELISE: *(to ARISTE)*. No, no; you are mistaken. You do not know the story, and the thing is not as you imagine.

ARISTE: How so, sister?

BELISE: Clitandre deceives you; it is with another that he is in love.

ARISTE: It is not with Henriette that he is in love? You are joking.

BELISE: No; I am telling the perfect truth.

ARISTE: He told me so himself.

BELISE: Doubtless.

ARISTE: You see me here, sister, commissioned by him to ask her of her father.

BELISE: Yes, I know.

ARISTE: And he besought me, in the name of his love, to hasten the time of an alliance so desired by him.

BELISE: Better and better. No more gallant subterfuge could have been employed. But let me tell you that Henriette is an excuse, an ingenious veil, a pretext, brother, to cover another flame, the mystery of which I know; and most willingly will I enlighten you both.

ARISTE: Since you know so much, sister, pray tell us whom he loves.

BELISE: You wish to know?

ARISTE: Yes; who is it?

BELISE: Me!

ARISTE: You!

BELISE: Myself.

ARISTE: Come, I say! sister!

BELISE: What do you mean by this "Come, I say"? And what is there so wonderful in what I tell you? I am handsome enough, I should think, to have more than one heart in subjection to my empire; and Dorante, Damis, Cléonte, and Lycidas show well enough the power of my charms.

ARISTE: Do those men love you?

BELISE: Yes; with all their might.

ARISTE: They have told you so?

BELISE: No one would take such a liberty; they have, up to the present time, respected me so much that they have never spoken to me of their love. But the dumb interpreters have done their office in offering their hearts and lives to me.

ARISTE: I hardly ever see Damis here.

BELISE: It is to show me a more respectful submission.

ARISTE: Dorante, with sharp words, abuses you everywhere.

BELISE: It is the transport of a jealous passion.

ARISTE: Cléonte and Lycidas are both married.

BELISE: It was the despair to which I had reduced their love.

ARISTE: Upon my word, sister, these are mere visions.

CHRYSALE: *(to BÉLISE).* You had better get rid of these idle fancies.

BELISE: Ah! idle fancies! They are idle fancies, you think. I have idle fancies! Really, "idle fancies" is excellent. I greatly rejoice at those idle fancies, brothers, and I did not know that I was addicted to idle fancies.

SCENE IV.
CHRYSALE, ARISTE.

CHRYSALE: Our sister is decidedly crazy.

ARISTE: It grows upon her every day. But let us resume the subject that brings me here. Clitandre asks you to give him Henriette in marriage. Tell me what answer we can make to his love.

CHRYSALE: Do you ask it? I consent to it with all my heart; and I consider his alliance a great honour.

ARISTE: You know that he is not wealthy, that....

CHRYSALE: That is a thing of no consequence. He is rich in virtue, and that is better than wealth. Moreover, his father and I were but one mind in two bodies.

ARISTE: Let us speak to your wife, and try to render her favourable to....

CHRYSALE: It is enough. I accept him for my son-in-law.

ARISTE: Yes; but to support your consent, it will not be amiss to have her agree to it also. Let us go....

CHRYSALE: You are joking? There is no need of this. I answer for my wife, and take the business upon myself.

ARISTE: But....

CHRYSALE: Leave it to me, I say, and fear nothing. I will go, and prepare her this moment.

ARISTE: Let it be so. I will go and see Henriette on the subject, and will return to know....

CHRYSALE: It is a settled thing, and I will go without delay and talk to my wife about it.

SCENE V.
CHRYSALE, MARTINE.

MARTINE: Just like my luck! Alas! they be true sayings, they be —"Give a dog a bad name and hang him," and—"One doesn't get fat in other folk's service."

CHRYSALE: What is it? What is the matter with you, Martine?

MARTINE: What is the matter?

CHRYSALE: Yes.

MARTINE: The matter is that I am sent away, Sir.

CHRYSALE: Sent away?

MARTINE: Yes; mistress has turned me out.

CHRYSALE: I don't understand; why has she?

MARTINE: I am threatened with a sound beating if I don't go.

CHRYSALE: No; you will stop here. I am quite satisfied with you. My wife is a little hasty at times, and I will not, no....

SCENE VI.
PHILAMINTE, BÉLISE, CHRYSALE, MARTINE.

PHILAMINTE: *(seeing MARTINE).* What! I see you here, you hussy! Quick, leave this place, and never let me set my eyes upon you again.

CHRYSALE: Gently.

PHILAMINTE: No; I will have it so.

CHRYSALE: What?

PHILAMINTE: I insist upon her going.

CHRYSALE: But what has she done wrong, that you wish her in this way to…?

PHILAMINTE: What! you take her part?

CHRYSALE: Certainly not.

PHILAMINTE: You side with her against me?

CHRYSALE: Oh! dear me, no; I only ask what she is guilty of.

PHILAMINTE: Am I one to send her away without just cause?

CHRYSALE: I do not say that; but we must, with servants….

PHILAMINTE: No; she must leave this place, I tell you.

CHRYSALE: Let it be so; who says anything to the contrary?

PHILAMINTE: I will have no opposition to my will.

CHRYSALE: Agreed.

PHILAMINTE: And like a reasonable husband, you should take my part against her, and share my anger.

CHRYSALE: So I do. *(Turning towards MARTINE.)* Yes; my wife is right in sending you away, baggage that you are; your crime cannot be forgiven.

MARTINE: What is it I have done, then?

CHRYSALE: *(aside).* Upon my word, I don't know.

PHILAMINTE: She is capable even now of looking upon it as nothing.

CHRYSALE: Has she caused your anger by breaking some looking-glass or some china?

PHILAMINTE: Do you think that I would send her away for that? And do you fancy that I should get angry for so little?

CHRYSALE: *(to MARTINE).* What is the meaning of this? *(To PHILAMINTE)* The thing is of great importance, then?

PHILAMINTE: Certainly; did you ever find me unreasonable?

CHRYSALE: Has she, through carelessness, allowed some ewer or silver dish to be stolen from us?

PHILAMINTE: That would be of little moment.

CHRYSALE: *(to MARTINE).* Oh! oh! I say, Miss! *(To PHILAMINTE)* What! has she shown herself dishonest?

PHILAMINTE: It is worse than that.

CHRYSALE: Worse than that?

PHILAMINTE: Worse.

CHRYSALE: *(to MARTINE).* How the deuce! you jade. *(To PHILAMINTE)* What! has she…?

PHILAMINTE: She has with unparalleled impudence, after thirty lessons, insulted my ear by the improper use of a low and vulgar word condemned in express terms by Vaugelas.

CHRYSALE: Is that…?

PHILAMINTE: What! In spite of our remonstrances to be always sapping the foundation of all knowledge—of grammar which rules even kings, and makes them, with a high hand, obey her laws.

CHRYSALE: I thought her guilty of the greatest crime.

PHILAMINTE: What! You do not think the crime unpardonable?

CHRYSALE: Yes, yes.

PHILAMINTE: I should like to see you excuse her.

CHRYSALE: Heaven forbid!

BELISE: It is really pitiful. All constructions are destroyed by her; yet she has a hundred times been told the laws of the language.

MARTINE: All that you preach there is no doubt very fine, but I don't understand your jargon, not I.

PHILAMINTE: Did you ever see such impudence? To call a language founded on reason and polite custom a jargon!

MARTINE: Provided one is understood, one speaks well enough, and all your fine speeches don't do me no good.

PHILAMINTE: You see! Is not that her way of speaking, don't do me no good!

BELISE: O intractable brains! How is it that, in spite of the trouble we daily take, we cannot teach you to speak with congruity? In putting not with no, you have spoken redundantly, and it is, as you have been told, a negative too many.

MARTINE: Oh my! I ain't no scholar like you, and I speak straight out as they speaks in our place.

PHILAMINTE: Ah! who can bear it?

BELISE: What a horrible solecism!

PHILAMINTE: It is enough to destroy a delicate ear.

BELISE: You are, I must acknowledge, very dull of understanding; they is in the plural number, and speaks is in the singular. Will you thus all your life offend grammar?

MARTINE: Who speaks of offending either gammer or gaffer?

PHILAMINTE: O heavens!

BELISE: The word grammar is misunderstood by you, and I have told you a hundred times where the word comes from.

MARTINE: Faith, let it come from Chaillot, Auteuil, or Pontoise, I care precious little.

BELISE: What a boorish mind! Grammar teaches us the laws of the verb and nominative case, as well as of the adjective and substantive.

MARTINE: Sure, let me tell you, Ma'am, that I don't know those people.

PHILAMINTE: What martyrdom!

BELISE: They are names of words, and you ought to notice how they agree with each other.

MARTINE: What does it matter whether they agree or fall out?

PHILAMINTE: *(to BÉLISE).* Goodness gracious! put an end to such a discussion. *(To CHRYSALE)* And so you will not send her away?

CHRYSALE: Oh! yes. *(Aside)* I must put up with her caprice, Go, don't provoke her, Martine.

PHILAMINTE: How! you are afraid of offending the hussy! you speak to her in quite an obliging tone.

CHRYSALE: I? Not at all. *(In a rough tone)* Go, leave this place. *(In a softer tone)* Go away, my poor girl.

SCENE VII.
PHILAMINTE, CHRYSALE, BÉLISE.

CHRYSALE: She is gone, and you are satisfied, but I do not approve of sending her away in this fashion. She answers very well for what she has to do, and you turn her out of my house for a trifle.

PHILAMINTE: Do you wish me to keep her for ever in my service, for her to torture my ears incessantly, to infringe all the laws of custom and reason, by a barbarous accumulation of errors of speech, and of garbled expressions tacked together with proverbs dragged out of the gutters of all the market-places?

BELISE: It is true that one sickens at hearing her talk; she pulls Vaugelas to pieces, and the least defects of her gross intellect are either pleonasm or cacophony.

CHRYSALE: What does it matter if she fails to observe the laws of Vaugelas, provided she does not fail in her cooking? I had much rather that while picking her herbs, she should join wrongly the nouns to the verbs, and repeat a hundred times a coarse or vulgar word, than that she should burn my roast, or put too much salt in my broth. I live on good soup, and not on fine language. Vaugelas does not teach how to make broth; and Malherbe and Balzac, so clever in learned words, might, in cooking, have proved themselves but fools.

PHILAMINTE: How shocking such a coarse speech sounds; and how unworthy of one who calls himself a man, to be always bent on material things, instead of rising towards those which are intellectual. Is that dross, the body, of importance enough to deserve even a passing thought? and ought we not to leave it far behind?

CHRYSALE: Well, my body is myself, and I mean to take care of it; dross if you like, but my dross is dear to me.

BELISE: The body and the mind, brother, exist together; but if you believe all the learned world, the mind ought to take precedence over the body, and our first care, our most earnest endeavour, must be to feed it with the juices of science.

CHRYSALE: Upon my word, if you talk of feeding your mind, you make use of but poor diet, as everybody knows; and you have no care, no solicitude for….

PHILAMINTE: Ah! Solicitude is unpleasant to my ear: it betrays strangely its antiquity.

BELISE: It is true that it is dreadfully starched and out of fashion.

CHRYSALE: I can bear this no longer. You will have me speak out, then? I will raise the mask, and discharge my spleen. Every one calls you mad, and I am greatly troubled at….

PHILAMINTE: Ah! what is the meaning of this?

CHRYSALE: *(to BÉLISE).* I am speaking to you, sister. The least solecism one makes in speaking irritates you; but you make strange ones in conduct. Your everlasting books do not satisfy me, and, except a big Plutarch to put my bands in you should burn all this useless lumber, and leave learning to the doctors of the town. Take away from the garret that long telescope, which is enough to frighten people, and a hundred other baubles which are offensive to the sight. Do not try to discover what is passing in the moon, and think a little more of what is happening at home, where we see everything going topsy-turvy. It is not right, and that too for many reasons, that a woman should study and know so much. To form the minds of her children to good manners, to make her household go well, to look after the servants, and regulate all expenses with economy, ought to be her principal study, and all her philosophy. Our fathers were much more sensible on this point: with them, a wife always knew enough when the extent of her genius enabled her to distinguish a doublet from a pair of breeches. She did not read, but she lived honestly; her family was the subject of all her learned conversation, and for hooks she had needles, thread, and a thimble, with which she worked at her daughter's trousseau. Women, in our days, are far from behaving thus: they must write and become authors. No science is too deep for them. It is worse in my house than anywhere else; the deepest secrets are understood, and everything is known except what should be known. Everyone knows how go the moon and the polar star, Venus, Saturn, and Mars, with which I have nothing to do. And in this vain knowledge, which they go so far to fetch, they know nothing of the soup of which I stand in need. My servants all wish to be learned, in order to please you; and all alike occupy themselves with anything but the work they have to do. Reasoning is the occupation of the whole house, and reasoning banishes all reason. One burns my roast while reading some story; another dreams of verses when I call for drink. In short, they all follow your example, and although I have servants, I am not served. One poor girl alone was left me, untouched by this villainous fashion; and now, behold, she is sent away with a huge clatter because she fails to speak Vaugelas. I tell you, sister, all this offends me, for as I have already said, it is to you I am speaking. I dislike to see all those Latin-mongers in my house, and particularly Mr. Trissotin. It is he who has turned your heads with his verses. All his talk is mere rubbish, and one is for ever trying to find out what he has said after he has done speaking. For my part I believe that he is rather cracked.

PHILAMINTE: What coarseness, O heavens! both in thought and language.

BELISE: Can there be a more gross assemblage of corpuscles, a mind composed of more vulgar atoms? Is it possible that I can come from the same blood? I hate myself for being of your race, and out of pure shame I abandon the spot.

SCENE VIII.
PHILAMINTE, CHRYSALE.

PHILAMINTE: Have you any other shaft ready?

CHRYSALE: I? No. Don't let us dispute any longer. I've done. Let's speak of something else. Your eldest daughter shows a dislike to marriage; in short, she is a philosopher, and I've nothing to say. She is under good management, and you do well by her. But her younger sister is of a different disposition, and I think it would be right to give Henriette a proper husband, who....

PHILAMINTE: It is what I have been thinking about, and I wish to speak to you of what I intend to do. This Mr. Trissotin on whose account we are blamed, and who has not the honour of being esteemed by you; is the man whom I have chosen to be her husband; and I can judge of his merit better than you can. All discussion is superfluous here, for I have duly resolved that it should be so. I will ask you also not to say a word of it to your daughter before I have spoken to her on the subject. I can justify my conduct, and I shall be sure to know if you have spoken to her.

SCENE IX.
ARISTE, CHRYSALE.

ARISTE: Well! your wife has just left, and I see that you must have had a talk together.

CHRYSALE: Yes.

ARISTE: And how did you succeed? Shall we have Henriette? Has she given her consent? Is the affair settled?

CHRYSALE: Not quite as yet.

ARISTE: Does she refuse?

CHRYSALE: No.

ARISTE: Then she hesitates?

CHRYSALE: Not in the least.

ARISTE: What then?

CHRYSALE: Well! she offers me another man for a son-in-law.

ARISTE: Another man for a son-in-law?

CHRYSALE: Yes.

ARISTE: What is his name?

CHRYSALE: Mr. Trissotin.

ARISTE: What! that Mr. Trissotin....

CHRYSALE: Yes, he who always speaks of verse and Latin.

ARISTE: And you have accepted him?

CHRYSALE: I? Heaven forbid!

ARISTE: What did you say to it?

CHRYSALE: Nothing. I am glad that I did not speak, and commit myself.

ARISTE: Your reason is excellent, and it is a great step towards the end we have in view. Did you not propose Clitandre to her?

CHRYSALE: No; for as she talked of another son-in-law, I thought it was better for me to say nothing.

ARISTE: Your prudence is to the last degree wonderful! Are you not ashamed of your weakness? How can a man be so poor-spirited as to let his wife have absolute power over him, and never dare to oppose anything she has resolved upon?

CHRYSALE: Ah! it is easy, brother, for you to speak; you don't know what a dislike I have to a row, and how I love rest and peace. My wife has a terrible disposition. She makes a great show of the name of philosopher, but she is not the less passionate on that account; and her philosophy, which makes her despise all riches, has no power over the bitterness of her anger. However little I oppose what she has taken into her head, I raise a terrible storm which lasts at least a week. She makes me tremble when she begins her outcries; I don't know where to hide myself. She is a perfect virago; and yet, in spite of her diabolical temper, I must call her my darling and my love.

ARISTE: You are talking nonsense. Between ourselves, your wife has absolute power over you only because of your own co-wardice. Her authority is founded upon your own weakness; it is from you she takes the name of mistress. You give way to her haughty manners, and suffer yourself to be led by the nose like a fool. What! you call yourself a man, and cannot for once make your wife obey you, and have courage enough to say, "I will have it so?" You will, without shame, see your daughter sacrificed to the mad visions with which the family is possessed? You will confer your wealth on a man because of half-a-dozen Latin words with which the ass talks big before them—a pedant whom your wife compliments at every turn with the names of wit and great philosopher whose verses were never equalled, whereas everybody knows that he is anything but all that. Once more I tell you, it is a shame, and you deserve that people should laugh at your cowardice.

CHRYSALE: Yes, you are right, and I see that I am wrong. I must pluck up a little more courage, brother.

ARISTE: That's right.

CHRYSALE: It is shameful to be so submissive under the tyranny of a woman.

ARISTE: Good.

CHRYSALE: She has abused my gentleness.

ARISTE: It is true.

CHRYSALE: My easy-going ways have lasted too long.

ARISTE: Certainly.

CHRYSALE: And to-day I will let her know that my daughter is my daughter, and that I am the master, to choose a husband for her according to my mind.

ARISTE: You are reasonable now, and as you should be.

CHRYSALE: You are for Clitandre, and you know where he lives; send him to me directly, brother.

ARISTE: I will go at once.

CHRYSALE: I have borne it too long. I will be a man, and set everybody at defiance.

ACT III.

SCENE I.
PHILAMINTE, ARMANDE, BÉLISE, TRISSOTIN, LÉPINE.

PHILAMINTE: Ah! Let us sit down here to listen comfortably to these verses; they should be weighed word by word.

ARMANDE: I am all anxiety to hear them.

BELISE: And I am dying for them.

PHILAMINTE: *(to TRISSOTIN).* Whatever comes from you is a delight to me.

ARMANDE: It is to me an unparalleled pleasure.

BELISE: It is a delicious repast offered to my ears.

PHILAMINTE: Do not let us languish under such pressing desires.

ARMANDE: Lose no time.

BELISE: Begin quickly and hasten our pleasure.

PHILAMINTE: Offer your epigram to our impatience.

TRISSOTIN: *(to PHILAMINTE).* Alas! it is but a new-born child, Madam, but its fate ought truly to touch your heart, for it was in your court-yard that I brought it forth, but a moment since.

PHILAMINTE: To make it dear to me, it is sufficient for me to know its father.

TRISSOTIN: Your approbation may serve it as a mother.

BELISE: What wit he has!

SCENE II.
HENRIETTE, PHILAMINTE, ARMANDE, BÉLISE, TRISSOTIN, LÉPINE.

PHILAMINTE: *(to HENRIETTE, who is going away).* Stop! why do you run away?

HENRIETTE: I fear to disturb such sweet intercourse.

PHILAMINTE: Come nearer, and with both ears share in the delight of hearing wonders.

HENRIETTE: I have little understanding for the beauties of authorship, and witty things are not in my line.

PHILAMINTE: No matter. Besides, I wish afterwards to tell you of a secret which you must learn.

TRISSOTIN: *(to HENRIETTE).* Knowledge has nothing that can touch you, and your only care is to charm everybody.

HENRIETTE: One as little as the other, and I have no wish....

BELISE: Ah! let us think of the new-born babe, I beg of you.

PHILAMINTE: *(to LÉPINE).* Now, little page, bring some seats for us to sit down. *(LÉPINE slips down.)* You senseless boy, how can you fall down after having learnt the laws of equilibrium?

BELISE: Do you not perceive, ignorant fellow, the causes of your fall, and that it proceeds from your having deviated from the fixed point which we call the centre of gravity?

LEPINE: I perceived it, Madam, when I was on the ground.

PHILAMINTE: *(to LÉPINE, who goes out).* The awkward clown!

TRISSOTIN: It is fortunate for him that he is not made of glass.

ARMANDE: Ah! wit is everything!

BELISE: It never ceases. *(They sit down.)*

PHILAMINTE: Serve us quickly your admirable feast.

TRISSOTIN: To satisfy, the great hunger which is here shown to me, a dish of eight verses seems but little; and I think that I should do well to join to the epigram, or rather to the madrigal, the ragout of a sonnet which, in the eyes of a princess, was thought to have a certain delicacy in it. It is throughout seasoned with Attic salt, and I think you will find the taste of it tolerably good.

ARMANDE: Ah! I have no doubt of it.

PHILAMINTE: Let us quickly give audience.

BELISE: *(interrupting TRISSOTIN each time he is about to read).* I feel, beforehand, my heart beating for joy. I love poetry to distraction, particularly when the verses are gallantly turned.

PHILAMINTE: If we go on speaking he will never be able to read.

TRISSOTIN: SONN....

BELISE: *(to HENRIETTE).* Be silent, my niece.

ARMANDE: Ah! let him read, I beg.

TRISSOTIN: SONNET TO THE PRINCESS URANIA ON HER FEVER.

> Your prudence fast in sleep's repose
> Is plunged; if thus superbly kind,
> A lodging gorgeously you can find
> For the most cruel of your foes—

BELISE: Ah! what a pretty beginning!

ARMANDE: What a charming turn it has!

PHILAMINTE: He alone possesses the talent of making easy verses.

ARMANDE: We must yield to prudence fast in sleep's repose is plunged.

BELISE: A lodging for the most cruel of your foes is full of charms for me.

PHILAMINTE: I like superbly and gorgeously; these two adverbs joined together sound admirably.

BELISE: Let us hear the rest.

TRISSOTIN:

> Your prudence fast in sleep's repose
> Is plunged; if thus superbly kind,
> A lodging gorgeously you can find
> For the most cruel of your foes

ARMANDE: Prudence asleep!

BELISE: Lodge one's enemy!

PHILAMINTE: Superbly and gorgeously!

TRISSOTIN:

> Will she, nill she, quick, out she goes!
> From your apartment richly lined,
> Where that ingrate's outrageous mind
> At your fair life her javelin throws.

BELISE: Ah! gently. Allow me to breathe, I beseech you.

ARMANDE: Give us time to admire, I beg.

PHILAMINTE: One feels, at hearing these verses, an indescribable something which goes through one's inmost soul, and makes one feel quite faint.

ARMANDE: Will she, nill she, quick, out she goes From your apartment richly lined. How prettily rich apartment is said here, and with what wit the metaphor is introduced!

PHILAMINTE: Will she, nill she, quick, out she goes! Ah! in what admirable taste that will she, nill she, is! To my mind the passage is invaluable.

ARMANDE: My heart is also in love with will she, nill she.

BELISE: I am of your opinion; will she, nill she, is a happy expression.

ARMANDE: I wish I had written it.

BELISE: It is worth a whole poem!

PHILAMINTE: But do you, like me, understand thoroughly the wit of it?

ARMANDE and BELISE: Oh! oh

PHILAMINTE: Will she, nill she, quick, out she goes! Although another should take the fever's part, pay no attention; laugh at the gossips; will she, nill she, quick, out she goes. Will she, nill she, will she, nill she. This will she, nill she, says a great deal more than it seems. I do not know if every one is like me, but I discover in it a hundred meanings.

BELISE: It is true that it says more than its size seems to imply.

PHILAMINTE: *(to TRISSOTIN).* But when you wrote this charming Will she, nill she, did you yourself understand all its energy? Did you realise all that it tells us, and did you then think that you were writing something so witty?

TRISSOTIN: Ah! ah!

ARMANDE: I have likewise the ingrate in my head; this ungrateful, unjust, uncivil fever that ill-treats people who entertain her.

PHILAMINTE: In short, both the stanzas are admirable. Let us come quickly to the triplets, I pray.

ARMANDE: Ah! once more, will she, nill she, I beg.

TRISSOTIN: Will she, nill she, quick, out she goes!

PHILAMINTE, ARMANDE and BELISE: Will she, nill she!

TRISSOTIN: From your apartment richly lined.

PHILAMINTE, ARMANDE and BELISE: Rich apartment!

TRISSOTIN: Where that ingrate's outrageous mind.

PHILAMINTE, ARMANDE and BELISE: That ungrateful fever!

TRISSOTIN: At your fair life her javelin throws.

PHILAMINTE: Fair life!

ARMANDE and BELISE: Ah!

TRISSOTIN:

> What! without heed for your high line,
> She saps your blood with care malign…

PHILAMINTE, ARMANDE and BELISE: Ah!

TRISSOTIN:

> Redoubling outrage night and day!
> If to the bath you take her down,
> Without a moment's haggling, pray,
> With your own hands the miscreant drown.

PHILAMINTE: Ah! it is quite overpowering.

BELISE: I faint.

ARMANDE: I die from pleasure.

PHILAMINTE: A thousand sweet thrills seize one.

ARMANDE: If to the bath you take her down,

BELISE: Without a moment's haggling, pray,

PHILAMINTE: With your own hands the miscreant drown. With your own hands, there, drown her there in the bath.

ARMANDE: In your verses we meet at each step with charming beauty.

BELISE: One promenades through them with rapture.

PHILAMINTE: One treads on fine things only.

ARMANDE: They are little lanes all strewn with roses.

TRISSOTIN: Then the sonnet seems to you....

PHILAMINTE: Admirable, new; and never did any one make anything more beautiful.

BELISE: *(to HENRIETTE).* What! my niece, you listen to what has been read without emotion! You play there but a sorry part!

HENRIETTE: We each of us play the best part we can, my aunt, and to be a wit does not depend on our will.

TRISSOTIN: My verses, perhaps, are tedious to you.

HENRIETTE: No. I do not listen.

TRISSOTIN: ON A CARRIAGE OF THE COLOUR OF AMARANTH GIVEN TO ONE OF HIS LADY FRIENDS.

PHILAMINTE: His titles have always something rare in them.

ARMANDE: They prepare one for a hundred flashes of wit.

TRISSOTIN:

> Love for his bonds so dear a price demands,
> E'en now it costs me more than half my lands,
> And when this chariot meets your eyes,
> Where so much gold emboss'd doth rise
> That people all astonished stand,
> And Laïs rides in triumph through the land...

PHILAMINTE: Ah! Laïs! what erudition!

BELISE: The cover is pretty, and worth a million.

TRISSOTIN:

> And when this chariot meets your eyes,
> Where so much gold emboss'd doth rise
> That people all astonished stand,
> And Laïs rides in triumph through the land,
> Say no more it is amaranth,
> Say rather it is o' my rent.

ARMANDE: Oh, oh, oh! this is beyond everything; who would have expected that?

PHILAMINTE: He is the only one to write in such taste.

BELISE: Say no more it is amaranth, say rather it is o' my rent! It can be declined; my rent; of my rent; to my rent; from my rent.

PHILAMINTE: I do not know whether I was prepossessed from the first moment I saw you, but I admire all your prose and verse whenever I see it.

TRISSOTIN: *(to PHILAMINTE).* If you would only show us something of your composition, we could admire in our turn.

PHILAMINTE: I have done nothing in verse; but I have reason to hope that I shall, shortly, be able, as a friend, to show you eight chapters of the plan of our Academy. Plato only touched on the subject when he wrote the treatise of his Republic; but I will complete the idea as I have arranged it on paper in prose. For, in short, I am truly angry at the wrong which is done us in regard to intelligence; and I will avenge the whole sex for the unworthy place which men assign us by confining our talents to trifles, and by shutting the door of sublime knowledge against us.

ARMANDE: It is insulting our sex too grossly to limit our intelligence to the power of judging of a skirt, of the make of a garment, of the beauties of lace, or of a new brocade.

BELISE: We must rise above this shameful condition, and bravely proclaim our emancipation.

TRISSOTIN: Every one knows my respect for the fairer sex, and that if I render homage to the brightness of their eyes, I also honour the splendour of their intellect.

PHILAMINTE: And our sex does you justice in this respect: but we will show to certain minds who treat us with proud contempt that women also have knowledge; that, like men, they can hold learned meetings—regulated, too, by better rules; that they wish to unite what elsewhere is kept apart, join noble language to deep learning, reveal nature's laws by a thousand experiments; and on all questions proposed, admit every party, and ally themselves to none.

TRISSOTIN: For order, I prefer peripateticism.

PHILAMINTE: For abstractions I love Platonism.

ARMANDE: Epicurus pleases me, for his tenets are solid.

BELISE: I agree with the doctrine of atoms: but I find it difficult to understand a vacuum, and I much prefer subtile matter.

TRISSOTIN: I quite agree with Descartes about magnetism.

ARMANDE: I like his vortices.

PHILAMINTE: And I his falling worlds.

ARMANDE: I long to see our assembly opened, and to distinguish ourselves by some great discovery.

TRISSOTIN: Much is expected from your enlightened know-ledge, for nature has hidden few things from you.

PHILAMINTE: For my part, I have, without boasting, already made one discovery; I have plainly seen men in the moon.

BELISE: I have not, I believe, as yet quite distinguished men, but I have seen steeples as plainly as I see you.

ARMANDE: In addition to natural philosophy, we will dive into grammar, history, verse, ethics, and politics.

PHILAMINTE: I find in ethics charms which delight my heart; it was formerly the admiration of great geniuses; but I give the preference to the Stoics, and I think nothing so grand as their founder.

ARMANDE: Our regulations in respect to language will soon be known, and we mean to create a revolution. Through a just or natural antipathy, we have each of us taken a mortal hatred to certain words, both verbs and nouns, and these we mutually abandon to each other. We are preparing sentences of death against them, we shall open our learned meetings by the proscription of the diverse words of which we mean to purge both prose and verse.

PHILAMINTE: But the greatest project of our assembly—a noble enterprise which transports me with joy, a glorious design which will be approved by all the lofty geniuses of posterity—is the cutting out of all those filthy syllables which, in the finest words, are a source of scandal: those eternal jests of the fools of all times; those nauseous commonplaces of wretched buffoons; those sources of infamous ambiguity, with which the purity of women is insulted.

TRISSOTIN: These are indeed admirable projects.

BELISE: You shall see our regulations when they are quite ready.

TRISSOTIN: They cannot fail to be wise and beautiful.

ARMANDE: We shall by our laws be the judges of all works; by our laws, prose and verse will both alike be submitted to us. No one will have wit except us or our friends. We shall try to find fault with everything, and esteem no one capable of writing but ourselves.

SCENE III
PHILAMINTE, BÉLISE, ARMANDE, HENRIETTE, TRISSOTIN, LÉPINE.

LEPINE: *(to TRISSOTIN).* Sir, there is a gentleman who wants to speak to you; he is dressed all in black, and speaks in a soft tone. *(They all rise.)*

TRISSOTIN: It is that learned friend who entreated me so much to procure him the honour of your acquaintance.

PHILAMINTE: You have our full leave to present him to us. *(TRISSOTIN goes out to meet VADIUS.)*

SCENE IV.
PHILAMINTE, BÉLISE, ARMANDE, HENRIETTE.

PHILAMINTE: *(to ARMANDE and BÉLISE).* At least, let us do him all the honours of our knowledge. *(To HENRIETTE, who is going)* Stop! I told you very plainly that I wanted to speak to you.

HENRIETTE: But what about?

PHILAMINTE: You will soon be enlightened on the subject.

SCENE V.
TRISSOTIN, VADIUS, PHILAMINTE, BÉLISE, ARMANDE, HENRIETTE.

TRISSOTIN: *(introducing VADIUS).* Here is the gentleman who is dying to see you. In presenting him I am not afraid, Madam, of being accused of introducing a profane person to you; he can hold his place among the wits.

PHILAMINTE: The hand which introduces him sufficiently proves his value.

TRISSOTIN: He has a perfect knowledge of the ancient authors, and knows Greek, Madam, as well as any man in France.

PHILAMINTE: *(to BÉLISE).* Greek! O heaven! Greek! He understands Greek, sister!

BELISE: *(to ARMANDE).* Ah, niece! Greek!

ARMANDE: Greek! ah! how delightful!

PHILAMINTE: What, Sir, you understand Greek? Allow me, I beg, for the love of Greek, to embrace you. *(VADIUS embraces also BÉLISE andARMANDE.)*

HENRIETTE: *(to VADIUS, who comes forward to embrace her)* Excuse me, Sir, I do not understand Greek. *(They sit down.)*

PHILAMINTE: I have a wonderful respect for Greek books.

VADIUS: I fear that the anxiety which calls me to render my homage to you to-day, Madam, may render me importunate. I may have disturbed some learned discourse.

PHILAMINTE: Sir, with Greek in possession, you can spoil nothing.

TRISSOTIN: Moreover, he does wonders in prose as well as in verse, and he could, if he chose, show you something.

VADIUS: The fault of authors is to burden conversation with their productions; to be at the Palais, in the walks, in the drawing-rooms, or at table, the indefatigable readers of their tedious verses. As for me, I think nothing more ridiculous than an author who goes about begging for praise, who, preying on the ears of the first comers, often makes them the martyrs of his night watches. I have never been guilty of such foolish conceit, and I am in that respect of the opinion of a Greek, who by an express law forbade all his wise men any unbecoming anxiety to read their works.—Here are some little verses for young lovers upon which I should like to have your opinion.

TRISSOTIN: Your verses have beauties unequalled by any others.

VADIUS: Venus and the Graces reign in all yours.

TRISSOTIN: You have an easy style, and a fine choice of words.

VADIUS: In all your writings one finds ithos and pathos.

TRISSOTIN: We have seen some eclogues of your composition which surpass in sweetness those of Theocritus and Virgil.

VADIUS: Your odes have a noble, gallant, and tender manner, which leaves Horace far behind.

TRISSOTIN: Is there anything more lovely than your canzonets?

VADIUS: Is there anything equal to the sonnets you write?

TRISSOTIN: Is there anything more charming than your little rondeaus?

VADIUS: Anything so full of wit as your madrigals?

TRISSOTIN: You are particularly admirable in the ballad.

VADIUS: And in bouts-rimés I think you adorable.

TRISSOTIN: If France could appreciate your value—

VADIUS: If the age could render justice to a lofty genius—

TRISSOTIN: You would ride in the streets in a gilt coach.

VADIUS: We should see the public erect statues to you. Hem... *(to TRISSOTIN).* It is a ballad; and I wish you frankly to....

TRISSOTIN: *(to VADIUS).* Have you heard a certain little sonnet upon the Princess Urania's fever?

VADIUS: Yes; I heard it read yesterday.

TRISSOTIN: Do you know the author of it?

VADIUS: No, I do not; but I know very well that, to tell him the truth, his sonnet is good for nothing.

TRISSOTIN: Yet a great many people think it admirable.

VADIUS: It does not prevent it from being wretched; and if you had read it, you would think like me.

TRISSOTIN: I know that I should differ from you altogether, and that few people are able to write such a sonnet.

VADIUS: Heaven forbid that I should ever write one so bad!

TRISSOTIN: I maintain that a better one cannot be made, and my reason is that I am the author of it.

VADIUS: You?

TRISSOTIN: Myself.

VADIUS: I cannot understand how the thing can have happened.

TRISSOTIN: It is unfortunate that I had not the power of pleasing you.

VADIUS: My mind must have wandered during the reading, or else the reader spoilt the sonnet; but let us leave that subject, and come to my ballad.

TRISSOTIN: The ballad is, to my mind, but an insipid thing; it is no longer the fashion, and savours of ancient times.

VADIUS: Yet a ballad has charms for many people.

TRISSOTIN: It does not prevent me from thinking it unpleasant.
VADIUS: That does not make it worse.
TRISSOTIN: It has wonderful attractions for pedants.
VADIUS: Yet we see that it does not please you.
TRISSOTIN: You stupidly give your qualities to others.

(They all rise.)

VADIUS: You very impertinently cast yours upon me.
TRISSOTIN: Go, you little dunce! you pitiful quill-driver!
VADIUS: Go, you penny-a-liner! you disgrace to the profession!
TRISSOTIN: Go, you book-maker, you impudent plagiarist!
VADIUS: Go, you pedantic snob!
PHILAMINTE: Ah! gentlemen, what are you about?
TRISSOTIN: *(to VADIUS).* Go, go, and make restitution to the Greeks and Romans for all your shameful thefts.
VADIUS: Go and do penance on Parnassus for having murdered Horace in your verses.
TRISSOTIN: Remember your book, and the little noise it made.
VADIUS: And you, remember your bookseller, reduced to the workhouse.
TRISSOTIN: My glory is established; in vain would you endeavour to shake it.
VADIUS: Yes, yes; I send you to the author of the 'Satires.'
TRISSOTIN: I, too, send you to him.
VADIUS: I have the satisfaction of having been honourably treated by him; he gives me a passing thrust, and includes me among several authors well known at the Palais; but he never leaves you in peace, and in all his verses you are exposed to his attacks.
TRISSOTIN: By that we see the honourable rank I hold. He leaves you in the crowd, and esteems one blow enough to crush you. He has never done you the honour of repeating his attacks, whereas he assails me separately, as a noble adversary against whom all his efforts are necessary; and his blows, repeated against me on all occasions, show that he never thinks himself victorious.
VADIUS: My pen will teach you what sort of man I am.
TRISSOTIN: And mine will make you know your master.
VADIUS: I defy you in verse, prose, Greek and Latin.

TRISSOTIN: Very well, we shall meet each other alone at Barbin's.

SCENE VI.
TRISSOTIN, PHILAMINTE, ARMANDE, BÉLISE, HENRIETTE.

TRISSOTIN: Do not blame my anger. It is your judgment I defend, Madam, in the sonnet he dares to attack.

PHILAMINTE: I will do all I can to reconcile you. But let us speak of something else. Come here, Henriette. I have for some time now been tormented at finding in you a want of intellectuality, but I have thought of a means of remedying this defect.

HENRIETTE: You take unnecessary trouble for my sake. I have no love for learned discourses. I like to take life easy, and it is too much trouble to be intellectual. Such ambition does not trouble my head, and I am perfectly satisfied, mother, with being stupid. I prefer to have only a common way of talking, and not to torment myself to produce fine words.

PHILAMINTE: That may be; but this stupidity wounds me, and it is not my intention to suffer such a stain on my family. The beauty of the face is a fragile ornament, a passing flower, a moment's brightness which only belongs to the epidermis; whereas that of the mind is lasting and solid. I have therefore been feeling about for the means of giving you the beauty which time cannot remove—of creating in you the love of knowledge, of insinuating solid learning into you; and the way I have at last determined upon is to unite you to a man full of genius; *(showing TRISSOTIN)* to this gentleman, in fact. It is he whom I intend you to marry.

HENRIETTE: Me, mother!

PHILAMINTE: Yes, you! just play the fool a little.

BELISE: *(to TRISSOTIN).* I understand you; your eyes ask me for leave to engage elsewhere a heart I possess. Be at peace, I consent. I yield you up to this union; it is a marriage which will establish you in society.

TRISSOTIN: *(to HENRIETTE).* In my delight, I hardly know what to tell you, Madam, and this marriage with which I am honoured puts me....

HENRIETTE: Gently, Sir; it is not concluded yet; do not be in such a hurry.

PHILAMINTE: What a way of answering! Do you know that if … but enough. You understand me. *(To TRISSOTIN)* She will obey. Let us leave her alone for the present.

SCENE VII.
HENRIETTE, ARMANDE.

ARMANDE: You see how our mother's anxiety for your welfare shines forth; she could not have chosen a more illustrious husband.…

HENRIETTE: If the choice is so good, why do you not take him for yourself?

ARMANDE: It is upon you, and not upon me, that his hand is bestowed.

HENRIETTE: I yield him up entirely to you as my elder Sister.

ARMANDE: If marriage seemed so pleasant to me as it seems to be to you, I would accept your offer with delight.

HENRIETTE: If I loved pedants as you do, I should think the match an excellent one.

ARMANDE: Although our tastes differ so in this case, you will still have to obey our parents, sister. A mother has full power over us, and in vain do you think by resistance to.…

SCENE VIII.
CHRYSALE, ARISTE, CLITANDRE, HENRIETTE, ARMANDE.

CHRYSALE: *(to HENRIETTE, as he presents CLITANDRE).* Now, my daughter, you must show your approval of what I do. Take off your glove, shake hands with this gentleman, and from henceforth in your heart consider him as the man I want you to marry.

ARMANDE: Your inclinations on this side are strong enough, sister.

HENRIETTE: We must obey our parents, sister; a father has full power over us.

ARMANDE: A mother should have a share of obedience.

CHRYSALE: What is the meaning of this?

ARMANDE: I say that I greatly fear you and my mother are not likely to agree on this point, and this other husband....

CHRYSALE: Be silent, you saucy baggage: philosophise as much as you please with her, and do not meddle with what I do. Tell her what I have done, and warn her that she is not to come and make me angry. Go at once!

SCENE IX.
CHRYSALE, ARISTE, HENRIETTE, CLITANDRE.

ARISTE: That's right; you are doing wonders!

CLITANDRE: What transport! what joy! Ah! how kind fortune is to me!

CHRYSALE: *(to CLITANDRE).* Come, take her hand and pass before us; take her to her room. Ah! what sweet caresses. *(to ARISTE)* How moved my heart is before this tenderness; it cheers up one's old age, and I can still remember my youthful loving days.

ACT IV.

SCENE I.
PHILAMINTE, ARMANDE.

ARMANDE: Yes, there was no hesitation in her; she made a display of her obedience, and her heart scarcely took time to hear the order. She seemed less to obey the will of her father than affect to set at defiance the will of her mother.

PHILAMINTE: I will soon show her to which of us two the laws of reason subject her wishes, and who ought to govern, mother or father, mind or body, form or matter.

ARMANDE: At least, they owed you the compliment of consulting you; and that little gentleman who resolves to become your son-in-law, in spite of yourself, behaves himself strangely.

PHILAMINTE: He has not yet reached the goal of his desires. I thought him well made, and approved of your love; but his manners were always unpleasant to me. He knows that I write a little, thank heaven, and yet he has never desired me to read anything to him.

SCENE II
ARMANDE, PHILAMINTE, CLITANDRE *(entering softly and listening unseen).*

ARMANDE: If I were you, I would not allow him to become Henriette's husband. It would be wrong to impute to me the least thought of speaking like an interested person in this matter, and false to think that the base trick he is playing me secretly vexes me. By the help of philosophy, my soul is fortified against such trials; by it we can rise above everything. But to see him treat you so, provokes me beyond all endurance. Honour requires you to resist his wishes, and he is not a man in whom you could find pleasure. In our talks together I never could see that he had in his heart any respect for you.

PHILAMINTE: Poor idiot!

ARMANDE: In spite of all the reports of your glory, he was always cold in praising you.

PHILAMINTE: The churl!

ARMANDE: And twenty times have I read to him some of your new productions, without his ever thinking them fine.

PHILAMINTE: The impertinent fellow!

ARMANDE: We were often at variance about it, and you could hardly believe what foolish things....

CLITANDRE *(to ARMANDE).* Ah! gently, pray. A little charity, or at least a little truthfulness. What harm have I done to you? and of what am I guilty that you should thus arm all your eloquence against me to destroy me, and that you should take so much trouble to render me odious to those whose assistance I need? Tell me why this great indignation? *(To PHILAMINTE)* I am willing to make you, Madam, an impartial judge between us.

ARMANDE: If I felt this great wrath with which you accuse me, I could find enough to authorise it. You deserve it but too well. A first love has such sacred claims over our hearts, that it would be better to lose fortune and renounce life than to love a second time. Nothing can be compared to the crime of changing one's vows, and every faithless heart is a monster of immorality.

CLITANDRE: Do you call that infidelity, Madam, which the haughtyiness of your mind has forced upon me? I have done nothing but obey the commands it imposed upon me; and if I offend you, you are the primary cause of the offence. At first your charms took entire possession of my heart. For two years I loved you with devoted love; there was no assiduous care, duty, respect, service, which I did not offer you. But all my attentions, all my cares, had no power over you. I found you opposed to my dearest wishes; and what you refused I offered to another. Consider then, if the fault is mine or yours. Does my heart run after change, or do you force me to it? Do I leave you, or do you not rather turn me away?

ARMANDE: Do you call it being opposed to your love, Sir, if I deprive it of what there is vulgar in it, and if I wish to reduce it to the purity in which the beauty of perfect love consists? You cannot for me keep your thoughts clear and disentangled from the commerce of sense; and you do not enter into the charms of that union of two hearts in which the body is ignored. You can only love with a gross and material passion; and in order to maintain in you the love I have created, you must have marriage, and all that follows. Ah! what strange love! How far great souls are from burning with these terrestrial flames! The senses have no share in all their ardour; their noble passion unites the hearts only, and treats all else as unworthy. Theirs is a flame pure and clear like a celestial fire. With this they breathe only sinless sighs, and never yield to base desires. Nothing impure is mixed in what they propose to themselves. They love for the sake of loving, and for nothing else. It is only to the soul that all their transports are directed, and the body they altogether forget.

CLITANDRE: Unfortunately, Madam, I feel, if you will forgive my saying so, that I have a body as well as a soul; and that I am too much attached to that body for me totally to forget it. I do not understand this separation. Heaven has denied me such philosophy, and my body and soul go together. There is nothing so beautiful, as you well say, as that purified love which is directed only to the heart, those unions of the soul and those tender thoughts so free from the commerce of sense. But such love is too refined for me. I am, as you observe, a little gross and material. I love with all my being; and, in the love that is given to me, I wish to include the whole person. This is not a subject for lofty self-denial; and, without wishing to wrong your noble sentiments, I see that in the world my method has a certain vogue; that marriage is somewhat the fashion, and passes for a tie honourable and tender enough to have made me wish to become your husband, without giving you cause to be offended at such a thought.

ARMANDE: Well, well! Sir, since without being convinced by what I say, your grosser feelings will be satisfied; since to reduce you to a faithful love, you must have carnal ties and material chains, I will, if I have my mother's permission, bring my mind to consent to all you wish.

CLITANDRE: It is too late; another has accepted before you and if I were to return to you, I should basely abuse the place of rest in which I sought refuge, and should wound the goodness of her to whom I fled when you disdained me.

PHILAMINTE: But, Sir, when you thus look forward, do you believe in my consent to this other marriage? In the midst of your dreams, let it enter your mind that I have another husband ready for her.

CLITANDRE: Ah! Madam, reconsider your choice, I beseech you; and do not expose me to such a disgrace. Do not doom me to the unworthy destiny of seeing myself the rival of Mr. Trissotin. The love of beaux esprits, which goes against me in your mind, could not have opposed to me a less noble adversary. There are people whom the bad taste of the age has reckoned among men of genius; but Mr. Trissotin deceives nobody, and everyone does justice to the writings he gives us. Everywhere but here he is esteemed at his just value; and what has made me wonder above all things is to see you exalt to the sky, stupid verses which you would have disowned had you yourself written them.

PHILAMINTE: If you judge of him differently from us, it is that we see him with other eyes than you do.

SCENE III.
TRISSOTIN, PHILAMINTE, ARMANDE, CLITANDRE.

TRISSOTIN: *(to PHILAMINTE).* I come to announce you great news. We have had a narrow escape while we slept. A world passed all along us, and fell right across our vortex. If in its way it had met with our earth, it would have dashed us to pieces like so much glass.

PHILAMINTE: Let us put off this subject till another season. This gentleman would understand nothing of it; he professes to cherish ignorance, and above all to hate intellect and knowledge.

CLITANDRE: This is not altogether the fact; allow me, Madam, to explain myself. I only hate that kind of intellect and learning which spoils people. These are good and beautiful in themselves; but I had rather be numbered among the ignorant than to see myself learned like certain people.

TRISSOTIN: For my part I do not believe, whatever opinion may be held to the contrary, that knowledge can ever spoil anything.

CLITANDRE: And I hold that knowledge can make great fools both in words and in deeds.

TRISSOTIN: The paradox is rather strong.

CLITANDRE: It would be easy to find proofs; and I believe without being very clever, that if reasons should fail, notable examples would not be wanting.

TRISSOTIN: You might cite some without proving your point.

CLITANDRE: I should not have far to go to find what I want.

TRISSOTIN: As far as I am concerned, I fail to see those notable examples.

CLITANDRE: I see them so well that they almost blind me.

TRISSOTIN: I believed hitherto that it was ignorance which made fools, and not knowledge.

CLITANDRE: You made a great mistake; and I assure you that a learned fool is more of a fool than an ignorant one.

TRISSOTIN: Common sense is against your maxims, since an ignorant man and a fool are synonymous.

CLITANDRE: If you cling to the strict uses of words, there is a greater connection between pedant and fool.

TRISSOTIN: Folly in the one shows itself openly.

CLITANDRE: And study adds to nature in the other.

TRISSOTIN: Knowledge has always its intrinsic value.

CLITANDRE: Knowledge in a pedant becomes impertinence.

TRISSOTIN: Ignorance must have great charms for you, since you so eagerly take up arms in its defence.

CLITANDRE: If ignorance has such charms for me, it is since I have met with learned people of a certain kind.

TRISSOTIN: These learned people of a certain kind may, when we know them well, be as good as other people of a certain other kind.

CLITANDRE: Yes, if we believe certain learned men; but that remains a question with certain people.

PHILAMINTE: *(to CLITANDRE.)* It seems to me, Sir....

CLITANDRE: Ah! Madam, I beg of you; this gentleman is surely strong enough without assistance. I have enough to do already with so strong an adversary, and as I fight I retreat.

ARMANDE: But the offensive eagerness with which your answers....

CLITANDRE: Another ally! I quit the field.

PHILAMINTE: Such combats are allowed in conversation, provided you attack no one in particular.

CLITANDRE: Ah! Madam, there is nothing in all this to offend him. He can bear raillery as well as any man in France; and he has supported many other blows without finding his glory tarnished by it.

TRISSOTIN: I am not surprised to see this gentleman take such a part in this contest. He belongs to the court; that is saying everything. The court, as every one well knows, does not care for learning; it has a certain interest in supporting ignorance. And it is as a courtier he takes up its defence.

CLITANDRE: Your are very angry with this poor court. The misfortune is great indeed to see you men of learning day after day declaiming against it; making it responsible for all your troubles; calling it to account for its bad taste, and seeing in it the scapegoat of your ill-success. Allow me, Mr. Trissotin, to tell you, with all the respect with which your name inspires me, that you would do well, your brethren and you, to speak of the court in a more moderate tone; that, after all, it is not so very stupid as all you gentlemen make it out to be; that it has good sense enough to appreciate everything; that some good taste can be acquired there; and that the common sense found there is, without flattery, well worth all the learning of pedantry.

TRISSOTIN: We See some effects of its good taste, Sir.

CLITANDRE: Where do you see, Sir, that its taste is so bad?

TRISSOTIN: Where, Sir! Do not Rasius and Balbus by their learning do honour to France? and yet their merit, so very patent to all, attracts no notice from the court.

CLITANDRE: I see whence your sorrow comes, and that, through modesty, you forbear, Sir, to rank yourself with these. Not to drag you in, tell me what your able heroes do for their country? What service do their writings render it that they should accuse the court of horrible injustice, and complain everywhere that it fails to pour down favours on their learned names? Their knowledge is of great moment to France! and the court stands in great need of the books they write! These wretched scribblers get it into their little heads that to be printed and bound in calf makes them at once important personages in the state; that with their pens they regulate the destiny of crowns; that at the least mention of their productions, pensions ought to be poured down upon them; that the eyes of the whole universe are fixed upon them, and the glory of their name spread everywhere! They think themselves prodigies of learning because they know what others have said before them; because for thirty years they have had eyes and ears, and have employed nine or ten thousand nights or so in cramming themselves with Greek and Latin, and in filling their heads with the indiscriminate plunder of all the old rubbish which lies scattered in books. They always seem intoxicated with their own knowledge, and for all merit are rich in importunate babble. Unskilful in everything, void of common sense, and full of absurdity and impertinence, they decry everywhere true learning and knowledge.

PHILAMINTE: You speak very warmly on the subject, and this transport shows the working of ill-nature in you. It is the name of rival which excites in your breast....

SCENE IV.
TRISSOTIN, PHILAMINTE, CLITANDRE, ARMANDE, JULIAN.

JULIAN: The learned gentleman who paid you a visit just now, Madam, and whose humble servant I have the honour to be, exhorts you to read this letter.

PHILAMINTE: However important this letter may be, learn, friend, that it is a piece of rudeness to come and interrupt a conversation, and that a servant who knows his place should apply first to the people of the household to be introduced.

JULIAN: I will note that down, Madam, in my book.

PHILAMINTE: *(reads).* "Trissotin boasts, Madam, that he is to marry your daughter. I give you notice that his philosophy aims only at your wealth, and that you would do well not to conclude this marriage before you have seen the poem which I am composing against him. While you are waiting for this portrait, in which I intend to paint him in all his colours, I send you Horace, Virgil, Terence, and Catullus, where you will find marked in the margin all the passages he has pilfered."... We

47

see there merit attacked by many enemies because of the marriage I have decided upon. But this general ill-feeling only prompts me to an action which will confound envy, and make it feel that whatever it does only hastens the end. *(To JULIAN)* Tell all this to your master; tell him also that in order to let him know how much value I set on his disinterested advice, and how worthy of being followed I esteem it, this very evening I shall marry my daughter to this gentleman *(showing TRISSOTIN)*.

SCENE V.
PHILAMINTE, ARMANDE, CLITANDRE.

PHILAMINTE: *(to CLITANDRE).* You, Sir, as a friend of the family, may assist at the signing of the contract, for I am willing to invite you to it. Armande, be sure you send for the notary, and tell your sister of my decision.

ARMANDE: There is no need of saying anything to my sister; this gentleman will be pretty sure to take the news to her, and try and dispose her heart to rebellion.

PHILAMINTE: We shall see who has most power over her, and whether I can bring her to a sense of her duty.

SCENE VI.
ARMANDE, CLITANDRE.

ARMANDE: I am very sorry to see, Sir, that things are not going quite according to your views.

CLITANDRE: I shall go and do all I can not to leave this serious anxiety upon your mind.

ARMANDE: I am afraid that your efforts will not be very successful.

CLITANDRE: You may perhaps see that your fears are without foundation.

ARMANDE: I hope it may be so.

CLITANDRE: I am persuaded that I shall have all your help.

ARMANDE: Yes, I will second you with all my power.

CLITANDRE: And I shall be sure to be most grateful.

SCENE VII.

CHRYSALE, ARISTE, HENRIETTE, CLITANDRE.

CLITANDRE: I should be most unfortunate without your assistance, Sir, for your wife has rejected my offer, and, her mind being prepossessed in favour of Trissotin, she insists upon having him for a son-in-law.

CHRYSALE: But what fancy is this that she has got into her head? Why in the world will she have this Mr. Trissotin?

ARISTE: It is because he has the honour of rhyming with Latin that he is carrying it off over the head of his rival.

CLITANDRE: She wants to conclude this marriage to-night.

CHRYSALE: To-night?

CLITANDRE: Yes, to-night.

CHRYSALE: Well! and this very night I will, in order to thwart her, have you both married.

CLITANDRE: She has sent for the notary to draw up the contract.

CHRYSALE: And I will go and fetch him for the one he must draw up.

CLITANDRE: And Henriette is to be told by her sister of the marriage to which she must look forward.

CHRYSALE: And I command her with full authority to prepare herself for this other alliance. Ah! I will show them if there is any other master but myself to give orders in the house. *(To HENRIETTE)* We will return soon. Now, come along with me, brother; and you also, my son-in-law.

HENRIETTE: *(to ARISTE).* Alas! try to keep him in this disposition.

ARISTE: I will do everything to serve your love.

SCENE VIII.

HENRIETTE, CLITANDRE.

CLITANDRE: However great may be the help that is promised to my love, my greatest hope is in your constancy.

HENRIETTE: You know that you may be sure of my love.

CLITANDRE: I see nothing to fear as long as I have that.

HENRIETTE: You see to what a union they mean to force me.

CLITANDRE: As long as your heart belongs entirely to me, I see nothing to fear.

HENRIETTE: I will try everything for the furtherance of our dearest wishes, and if after all I cannot be yours, there is a sure retreat I have resolved upon, which will save me from belonging to any one else.

CLITANDRE: May Heaven spare me from ever receiving from you that proof of your love.

ACT V.

SCENE I.
HENRIETTE, TRISSOTIN.

HENRIETTE: It is about the marriage which my mother has set her heart upon that I wish, Sir, to speak privately to you; and I thought that, seeing how our home is disturbed by it, I should be able to make you listen to reason. You are aware that with me you will receive a considerable dowry; but money, which we see so many people esteem, has no charms worthy of a philosopher; and contempt for wealth and earthly grandeur should not show itself in your words only.

TRISSOTIN: Therefore it is not that which charms me in you; but your dazzling beauty, your sweet and piercing eyes, your grace, your noble air—these are the wealth, the riches, which have won for you my vows and love; it is of those treasures only that I am enamoured.

HENRIETTE: I thank you for your generous love; I ought to feel grateful and to respond to it; I regret that I cannot; I esteem you as much as one can esteem another; but in me I find an obstacle to loving you. You know that a heart cannot be given to two people, and I feel that Clitandre has taken entire possession of mine. I know that he has much less merit than you, that I have not fit discrimination for the choice of a husband, and that with your many talents yon ought to please me. I see that I am wrong, but I cannot help it; and all the power that reason has over me is to make me angry with myself for such blindness.

TRISSOTIN: The gift of your hand, to which I am allowed to aspire, will give me the heart possessed by Clitandre; for by a thousand tender cares I have reason to hope that I shall succeed in making myself loved.

HENRIETTE: No; my heart is bound to its first love, and cannot be touched by your cares and attention. I explain myself plainly with you, and my confession ought in no way to hurt your feelings. The love which springs up in the heart is not, as you know, the effect of merit, but is partly decided by caprice;

and oftentimes, when some one pleases us, we can barely find the reason. If choice and wisdom guided love, all the tenderness of my heart would be for you; but love is not thus guided. Leave me, I pray, to my blindness; and do not profit by the violence which, for your sake, is imposed on my obedience. A man of honour will owe nothing to the power which parents have over us; he feels a repugnance to exact a self-sacrifice from her he loves, and will not obtain a heart by force. Do not encourage my mother to exercise, for your sake, the absolute power she has over me. Give up your love for me, and carry to another the homage of a heart so precious as yours.

TRISSOTIN: For this heart to satisfy you, you must impose upon it laws it can obey. Could it cease to love you, Madam, unless you ceased to be loveable, and could cease to display those celestial charms…

HENRIETTE: Ah! Sir, leave aside all this trash; you are encumbered with so many Irises, Phyllises, Amaranthas, which everywhere in your verses you paint as charming, and to whom you swear such love, that….

TRISSOTIN: It is the mind that speaks, and not the heart. With them it is only the poet that is in love; but it is in earnest that I love the adorable Henriette.

HENRIETTE: Ah, Sir, I beg of you….

TRISSOTIN: If I offend you, my offence is not likely to cease. This love, ignored by you to this day, will be of eternal duration. Nothing can put a stop to its delightful transports; and although your beauty condemns my endeavours, I cannot refuse the help of a mother who wishes to crown such a precious flame. Provided I succeed in obtaining such great happiness, provided I obtain your hand, it matters little to me how it comes to pass.

HENRIETTE: But are you aware, Sir, that you risk more than you think by using violence; and to be plain with you, that it is not safe to marry a girl against her wish, for she might well have recourse to a certain revenge that a husband should fear.

TRISSOTIN: Such a speech has nothing that can make me alter my purpose. A philosopher is prepared against every event. Cured by reason of all vulgar weaknesses, he rises above these things, and is far from minding what does not depend on him.

HENRIETTE: Truly, Sir, I am delighted to hear you; and I had no idea that philosophy was so capable of teaching men to bear such accidents with constancy. This wonderful strength of mind deserves to have a fit subject to illustrate it, and to find one who may take pleasure in giving it an occasion for its full display. As, however, to say the truth, I do not feel equal to the task, I will leave it to another; and, between ourselves, I assure you that I renounce altogether the happiness of seeing you my husband.

TRISSOTIN: *(going).* We shall see by-and-by how the affair will end.

(In the next room, close at hand, is the notary waiting.)

SCENE II.
CHRYSALE, CLITANDRE, HENRIETTE.

CHRYSALE: I am glad, my daughter, to see you; come here and fulfill your duty, by showing obedience to the will of your father. I will teach your mother how to behave, and, to defy her more fully, here is Martine, whom I have brought back to take her old place in the house again.

HENRIETTE: Your resolution deserves praise. I beg of you, father, never to change the disposition you are in. Be firm in what you have resolved, and do not suffer yourself to be the dupe of your own good-nature. Do not yield; and I pray you to act so as to hinder my mother from having her own way.

CHRYSALE: How! Do you take me for a booby?

HENRIETTE: Heaven forbid!

CHRYSALE: Am I a fool, pray?

HENRIETTE: I do not say that.

CHRYSALE: Am I thought unfit to have the decision of a man of sense?

HENRIETTE: No, father.

CHRYSALE: Ought I not at my age to know how to be master at home?

HENRIETTE: Of course.

CHRYSALE: Do you think me weak enough to allow my wife to lead me by the nose?

HENRIETTE: Oh dear, no, father.

CHRYSALE: Well, then, what do you mean? You are a nice girl to speak to me as you do!

HENRIETTE: If I have displeased you, father, I have done so unintentionally.

CHRYSALE: My will is law in this place.

HENRIETTE: Certainly, father.

CHRYSALE: No one but myself has in this house a right to command.

HENRIETTE: Yes, you are right, father.

CHRYSALE: It is I who hold the place of chief of the family.

HENRIETTE: Agreed.

CHRYSALE: It is I who ought to dispose of my daughter's hand.

HENRIETTE: Yes, indeed, father.

CHRYSALE: Heaven has given me full power over you.

HENRIETTE: No one, father, says anything to the contrary.

CHRYSALE: And as to choosing a husband, I will show you that it is your father, and not your mother, whom you have to obey.

HENRIETTE: Alas! in that you respond to my dearest wish. Exact obedience to you is my earnest wish.

CHRYSALE: We shall see if my wife will prove rebellious to my will.

CLITANDRE: Here she is, and she brings the notary with her.

CHRYSALE: Back me up, all of you.

MARTINE: Leave that to me; I will take care to encourage you, if need be.

SCENE III.
PHILAMINTE, BÉLISE, ARMANDE, TRISSOTIN, A
NOTARY, CHRYSALE, CLITANDRE, HENRIETTE,
MARTINE.

PHILAMINTE: *(to the NOTARY).* Can you not alter your barbarous style, and give us a contract couched in noble language?

NOTARY: Our style is very good, and I should be a blockhead, Madam, to try and change a single word.

BELISE: Ah! what barbarism in the very midst of France! But yet, Sir, for learning's sake, allow us, instead of crowns, livres, and francs, to have the dowry expressed in minae and talents, and to express the date in Ides and Kalends.

NOTARY: I, Madam? If I were to do such a thing, all my colleagues would hiss me.

PHILAMINTE: It is useless to complain of all this barbarism. Come, Sir, sit down and write. *(Seeing MARTINE)* Ah! this impudent hussy dares to show herself here again! Why was she brought back, I should like to know?

CHRYSALE: We will tell you by-and-by; we have now something else to do.

NOTARY: Let us proceed with the contract. Where is the future bride?

PHILAMINTE: It is the younger daughter I give in marriage.

NOTARY: Good.

CHRYSALE: *(showing HENRIETTE).* Yes, Sir, here she is; her name is Henriette.

NOTARY: Very well; and the future bridegroom?

PHILAMINTE: *(showing TRISSOTIN).* This gentleman is the husband I give her.

CHRYSALE: *(showing CLITANDRE).* And the husband I wish her to marry is this gentleman.

NOTARY: Two husbands! Custom does not allow of more than one.

PHILAMINTE: *(to the NOTARY).* What is it that is stopping you? Put down Mr. Trissotin as my son-in-law.

CHRYSALE: For my son-in-law put down Mr. Clitandre.

NOTARY: Try and agree together, and come to a quiet decision as to who is to be the future husband.

PHILAMINTE: Abide, Sir, abide by my own choice.

CHRYSALE: Do, Sir, do according to my will.

NOTARY: Tell me which of the two I must obey.

PHILAMINTE: *(to CHRYSALE).* What! you will go against my wishes.

CHRYSALE: I cannot allow my daughter to be sought after only because of the wealth which is in my family.

PHILAMINTE: Really! as if anyone here thought of your wealth, and as if it were a subject worthy the anxiety of a wise man.

CHRYSALE: In short, I have fixed on Clitandre.

PHILAMINTE: *(showing TRISSOTIN).* And I am decided that for a husband she shall have this gentleman. My choice shall be followed; the thing is settled.

CHRYSALE: Heyday! you assume here a very high tone.

MARTINE: 'Tisn't for the wife to lay down the law, and I be one to give up the lead to the men in everything.

CHRYSALE: That is well said.

MARTINE: If my discharge was as sure as a gun, what I says is, that the hen hadn't ought to be heard when the cock's there.

CHRYSALE: Just so.

MARTINE: And we all know that a man is always chaffed, when at home his wife wears the breeches.

CHRYSALE: It is perfectly true.

MARTINE: I says that, if I had a husband, I would have him be the master of the house. I should not care a bit for him if he played the henpecked husband; and if I resisted him out of caprice, or if I spoke too loud, I should think it quite right if, with a couple of boxes on the ear, he made me pitch it lower.

CHRYSALE: You speak as you ought.

MARTINE: Master is quite right to want a proper husband for his daughter.

CHRYSALE: Certainly.

MARTINE: Why should he refuse her Clitandre, who is young and handsome, in order to give her a scholar, who is always splitting hairs about something? She wants a husband and not a pedagogue, and as she cares neither for Greek nor Latin, she has no need of Mr. Trissotin.

CHRYSALE: Excellent.

PHILAMINTE: We must suffer her to chatter on at her ease.

MARTINE: Learned people are only good to preach in a pulpit, and I have said a thousand times that I wouldn't have a learned man for my husband. Learning is not at all what is wanted in a household. Books agree badly with marriage, and if ever I consent to engage myself to anybody, it will be to a husband who has no other book but me, who doesn't know a from b— no offence to you, Madam—and, in short, who would be clever only for his wife.

PHILAMINTE: *(to CHRYSALE).* Is it finished? and have I listened patiently enough to your worthy interpreter?

CHRYSALE: She has only said the truth.

PHILAMINTE: And I, to put an end to this dispute, will have my wish obeyed. *(Showing TRISSOTIN)* Henriette and this gentleman shall be united at once. I have said it, and I will have it so. Make no reply; and if you have given your word to Clitandre, offer him her elder sister.

CHRYSALE: Ah! this is a way out of the difficulty. *(To HENRIETTE and CLITANDRE)* Come, do you consent?

HENRIETTE: How! father…!

CLITANDRE: *(to CHRYSALE).* What! Sir…!

BELISE: Propositions more to his taste might be made. But we are establishing a kind of love which must be as pure as the morning-star; the thinking substance is admitted, but not the material substance.

SCENE IV.
ARISTE, CHRYSALE, PHILAMINTE, BÉLISE, HENRIETTE, ARMANDE, TRISSOTIN, A NOTARY, CLITANDRE, MARTINE.

ARISTE: I am sorry to have to trouble this happy ceremony by the sad tidings of which I am obliged to be bearer. These two letters make me bring news which have made me feel grievously for you. *(To PHILAMINTE)* One letter is for you, and comes from your attorney. *(To CHRYSALE)* The other comes from Lyons.

PHILAMINTE: What misfortune can be sent us worthy of troubling us?

ARISTE: You can read it in this letter.

PHILAMINTE: "Madam, I have asked your brother to give you this letter; it will tell you news which I did not dare to come and tell you myself. The great negligence you have shown in your affairs has been the cause that the clerk of your attorney has not forewarned me, and you have altogether lost the lawsuit which you ought to have gained."

CHRYSALE: *(to PHILAMINTE).* Your lawsuit lost!

PHILAMINTE: *(to CHRYSALE).* You seem very much upset; my heart is in no way troubled by such a blow. Show, show like me, a less vulgar mind wherewith to brave the ills of fortune. "Your want of care will cost you forty thousand crowns, and you are condemned to pay this sum with all costs." Condemned? Ah! this is a shocking word, and only fit for criminals.

ARISTE: It is the wrong word, no doubt, and you, with reason, protest against it. It should have been, "You are desired by an order of the court to pay immediately forty thousand crowns and costs."

PHILAMINTE: Let us see the other.

CHRYSALE: "Sir, the friendship which binds me to your brother prompts me to take a lively interest in all that concerns you. I know that you had placed your fortune entirely in the hands of Argante and Damon, and I acquaint you with the news that they have both failed." O Heaven! to lose everything thus in a moment!

PHILAMINTE: *(to CHRYSALE.)* Ah! what a shameful outburst Fic! For the truly wise there is no fatal change of fortune, and, losing all, he still remains himself. Let us finish the business we have in hand; and please cast aside your sorrow. *(Showing TRISSOTIN)* His wealth will be sufficient for us and for him.

TRISSOTIN: No, Madam; cease, I pray you, from pressing this affair further. I see that everybody is opposed to this marriage, and I have no intention of forcing the wills of others.

PHILAMINTE: This reflection, Sir, comes very quickly after our reverse of fortune.

TRISSOTIN: I am tired at last of so much resistance, and prefer to relinquish all attempts at removing these obstacles. I do not wish for a heart that will not surrender itself.

PHILAMINTE: I see in you, and that not to your honour, what I have hitherto refused to believe.

TRISSOTIN: You may see whatever you please, and it matters little to me how you take what you see. I am not a man to put up with the disgrace of the refusals with which I have been insulted here. I am well worthy of more consideration, and whoever thinks otherwise, I am her humble servant. *(Exit.)*

SCENE V.
ARISTE, CHRYSALE, PHILAMINTE, BÉLISE, ARMANDE, HENRIETTE, CLITANDRE, A NOTARY, MARTINE.

PHILAMINTE: How plainly he has disclosed his mercenary soul, and how little like a philosopher he has acted.

CLITANDRE: I have no pretension to being one; but, Madam, I will link my destiny to yours, and I offer you, with myself, all that I possess.

PHILAMINTE: Yon delight me, Sir, by this generous action, and I will reward your love. Yes, I grant Henriette to the eager affection....

HENRIETTE: No, mother. I have altered my mind; forgive me if now I resist your will.

CLITANDRE: What! do you refuse me happiness, and now that I see everybody for me....

HENRIETTE: I know how little you possess, Clitandre; and I always desired you for a husband when, by satisfying my most ardent wishes, I saw that our marriage would improve your fortune. But in the face of such reverses, I love you enough not to burden you with our adversity.

CLITANDRE: With you any destiny would be happiness, without you misery.

HENRIETTE: Love in its ardour generally speaks thus. Let us avoid the torture of vexatious recriminations. Nothing irritates such a tie more than the wretched wants of life. After a time we accuse each other of all the sorrows that follow such an engagement.

ARISTE: *(to HENRIETTE).* Is what you have just said the only reason which makes you refuse to marry Clitandre?

HENRIETTE: Yes; otherwise you would see me ready to fly to this union with all my heart.

ARISTE: Suffer yourself, then, to be bound by such gentle ties. The news I brought you was false. It was a stratagem, a happy thought I had to serve your love by deceiving my sister, and by showing her what her philosopher would prove when put to the test.

CHRYSALE: Heaven be praised!

PHILAMINTE: I am delighted at heart for the vexation which this cowardly deserter will feel. The punishment of his sordid avarice will be to see in what a splendid manner this match will be concluded.

CHRYSALE: *(to CLITANDRE).* I told you that you would marry her.

ARMANDE: *(to PHILAMINTE).* So, then, you sacrifice me to their love?

PHILAMINTE: It will not be to sacrifice you; you have the support of your philosophy, and you can with a contented mind see their love crowned.

BELISE: Let him take care, for I still retain my place in his heart. Despair often leads people to conclude a hasty marriage, of which they repent ever after.

CHRYSALE: *(to the NOTARY).* Now, Sir, execute my orders, and draw up the contract in accordance with what I said.

CURTAIN

Made in United States
North Haven, CT
19 December 2023

46225848R00036